We Swear for

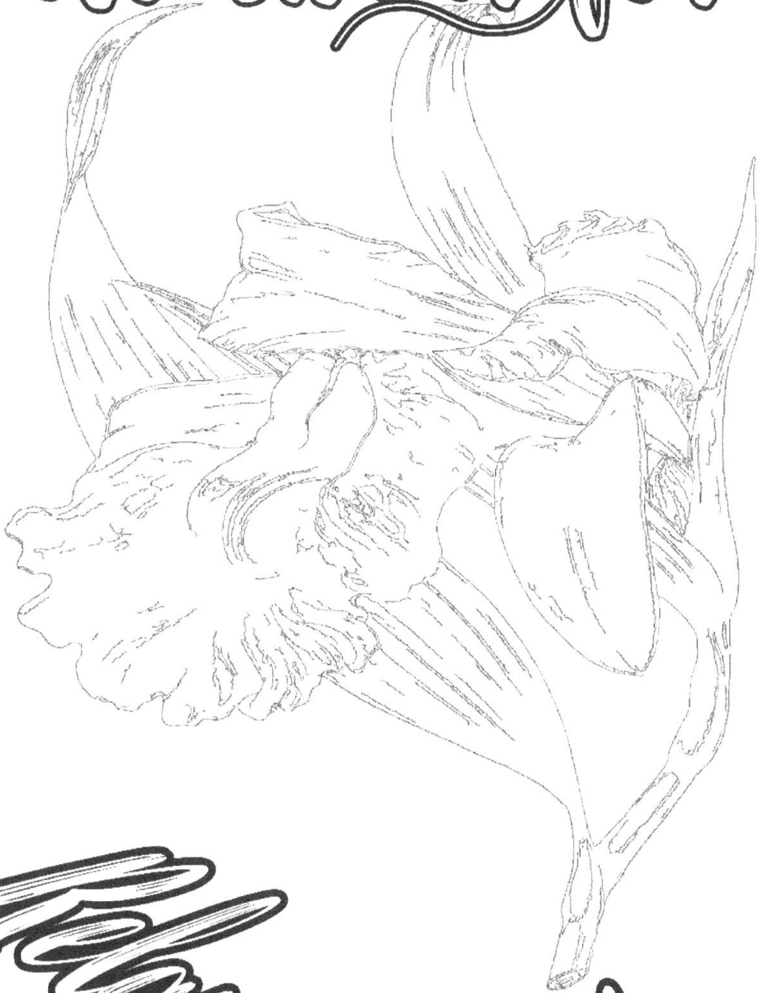

Relaxing & Releasing

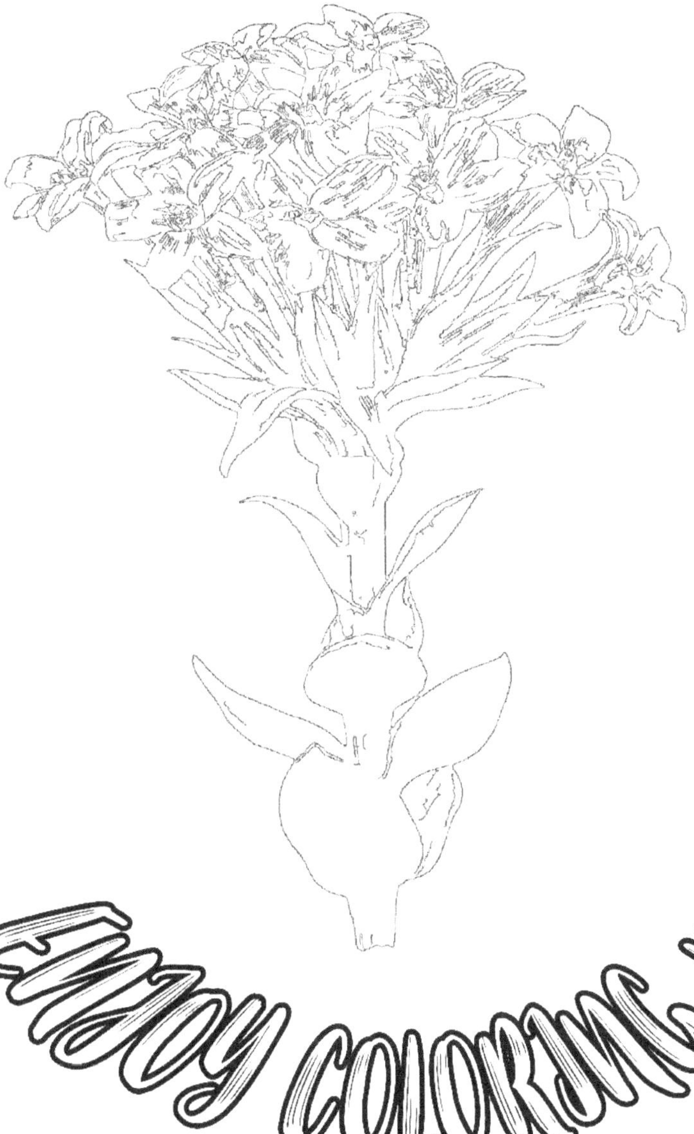

ENJOY COLORING !!!

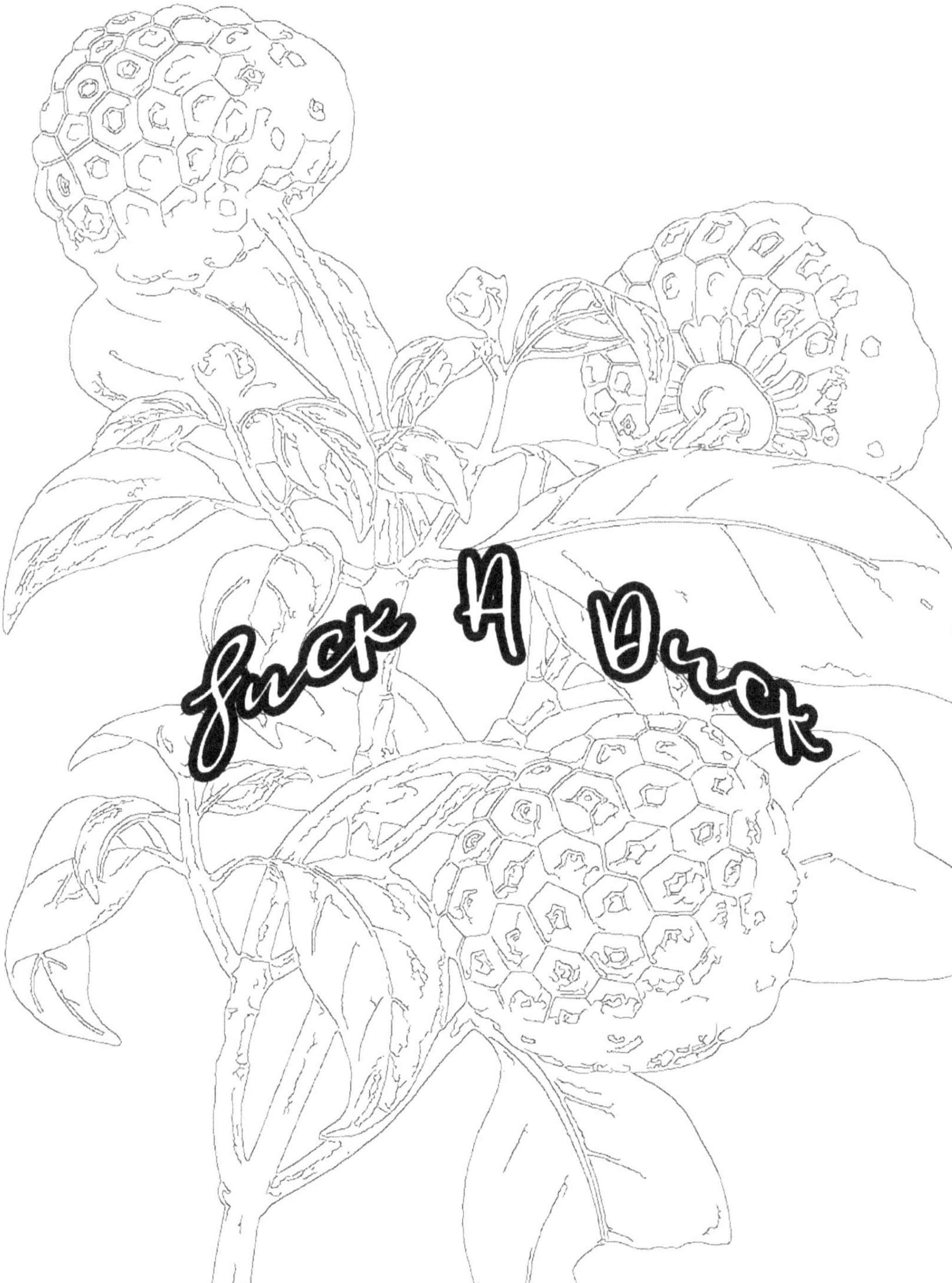
fuck A Duck

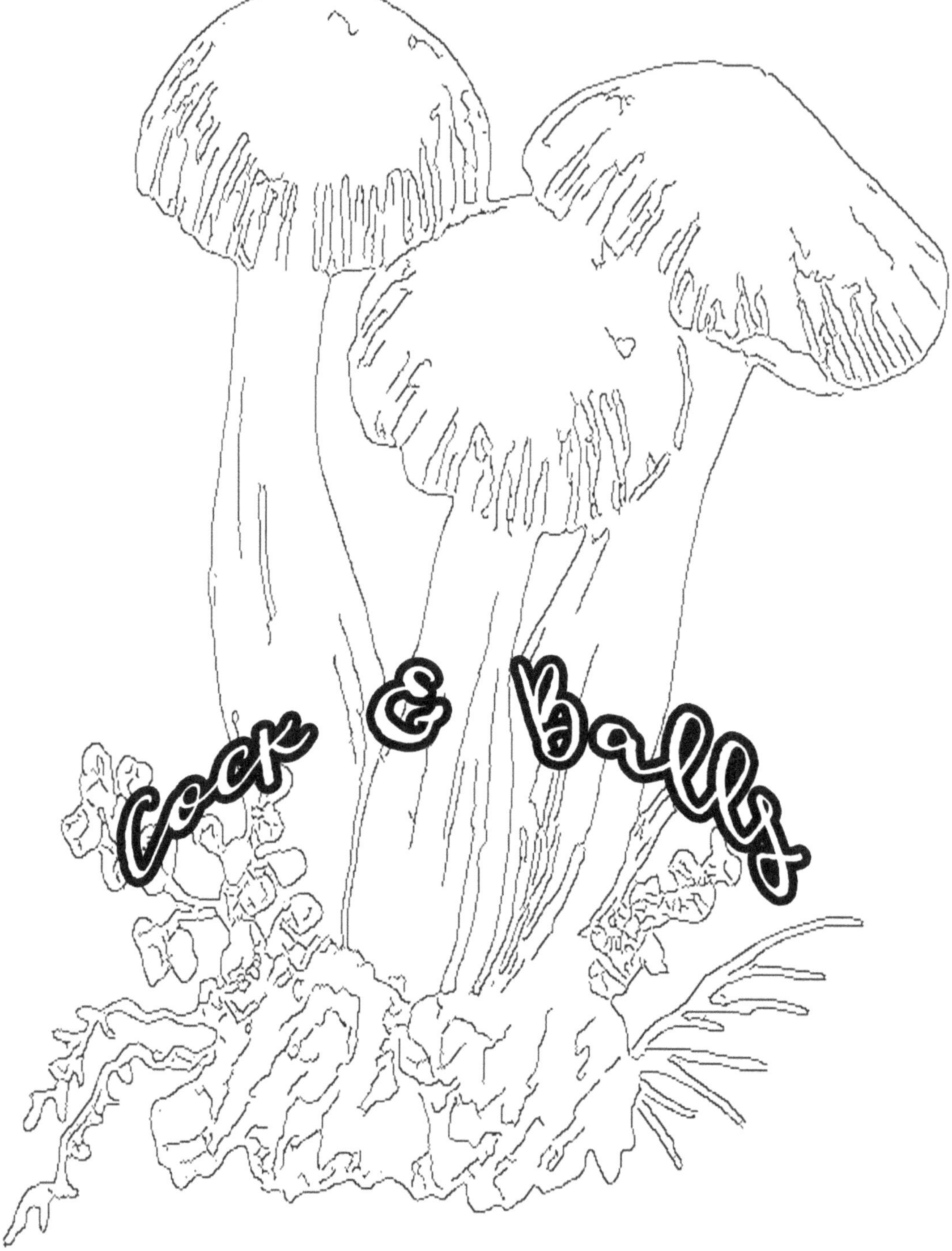
Cock & Balls

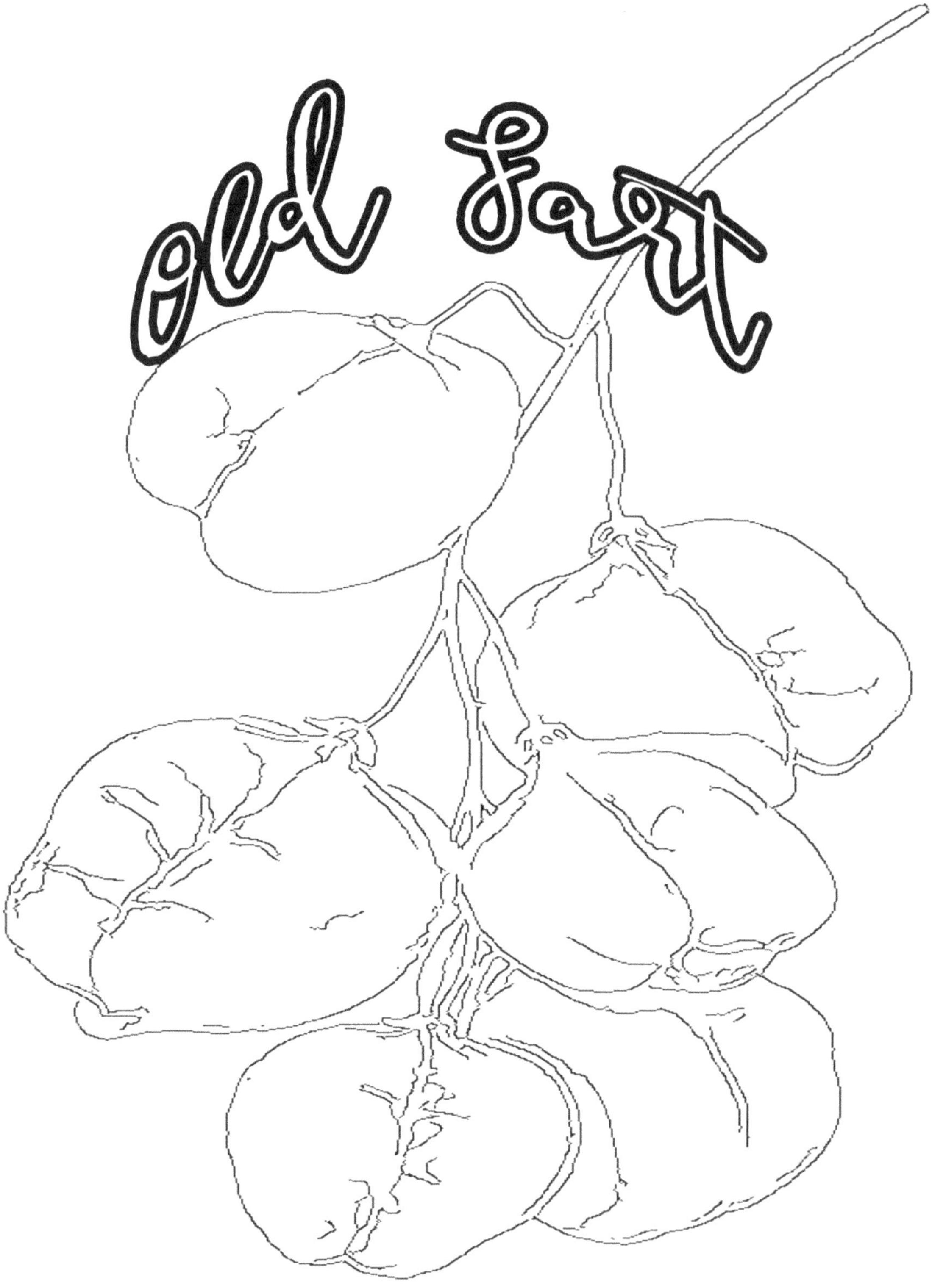
old fart

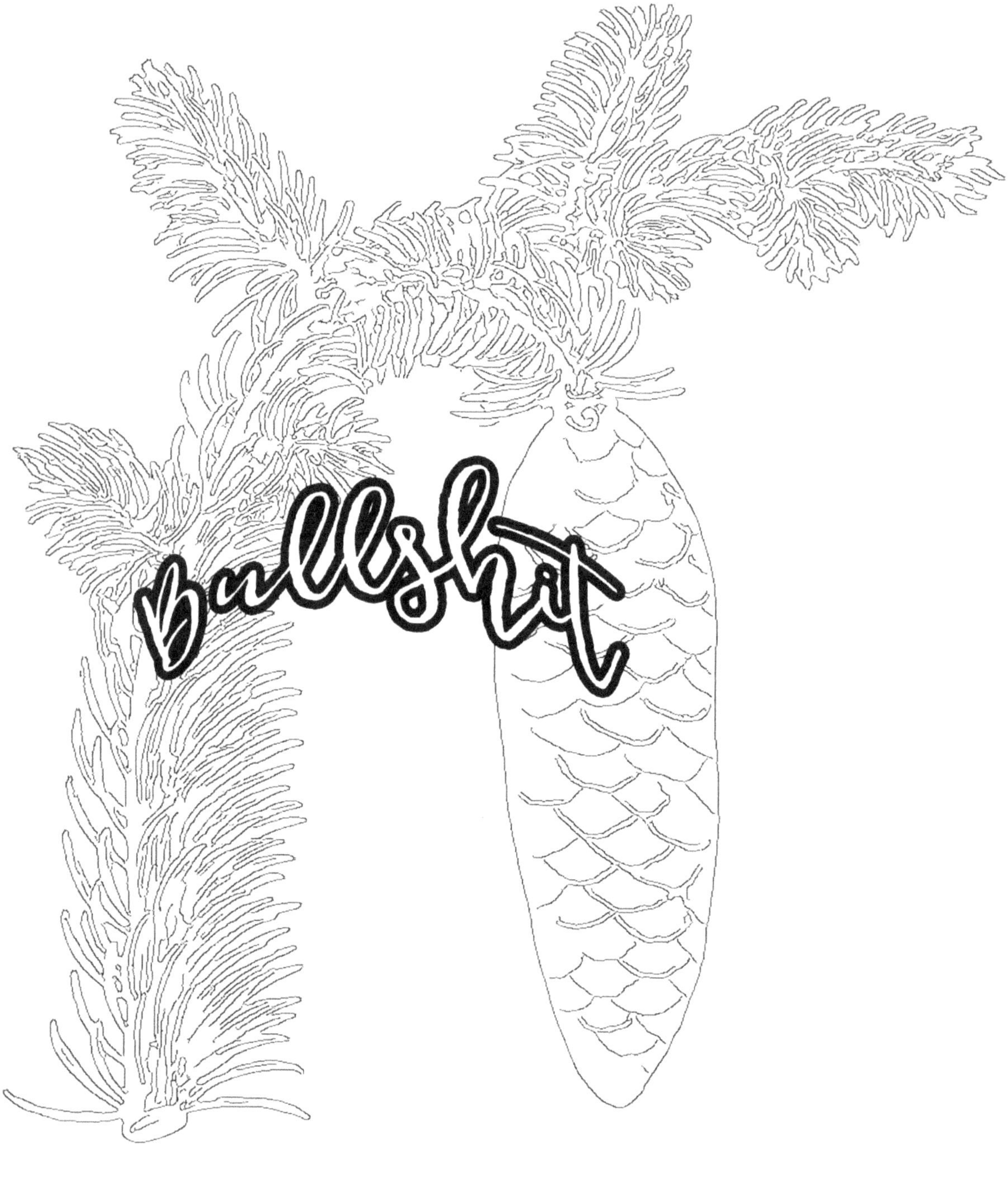
Bullshit

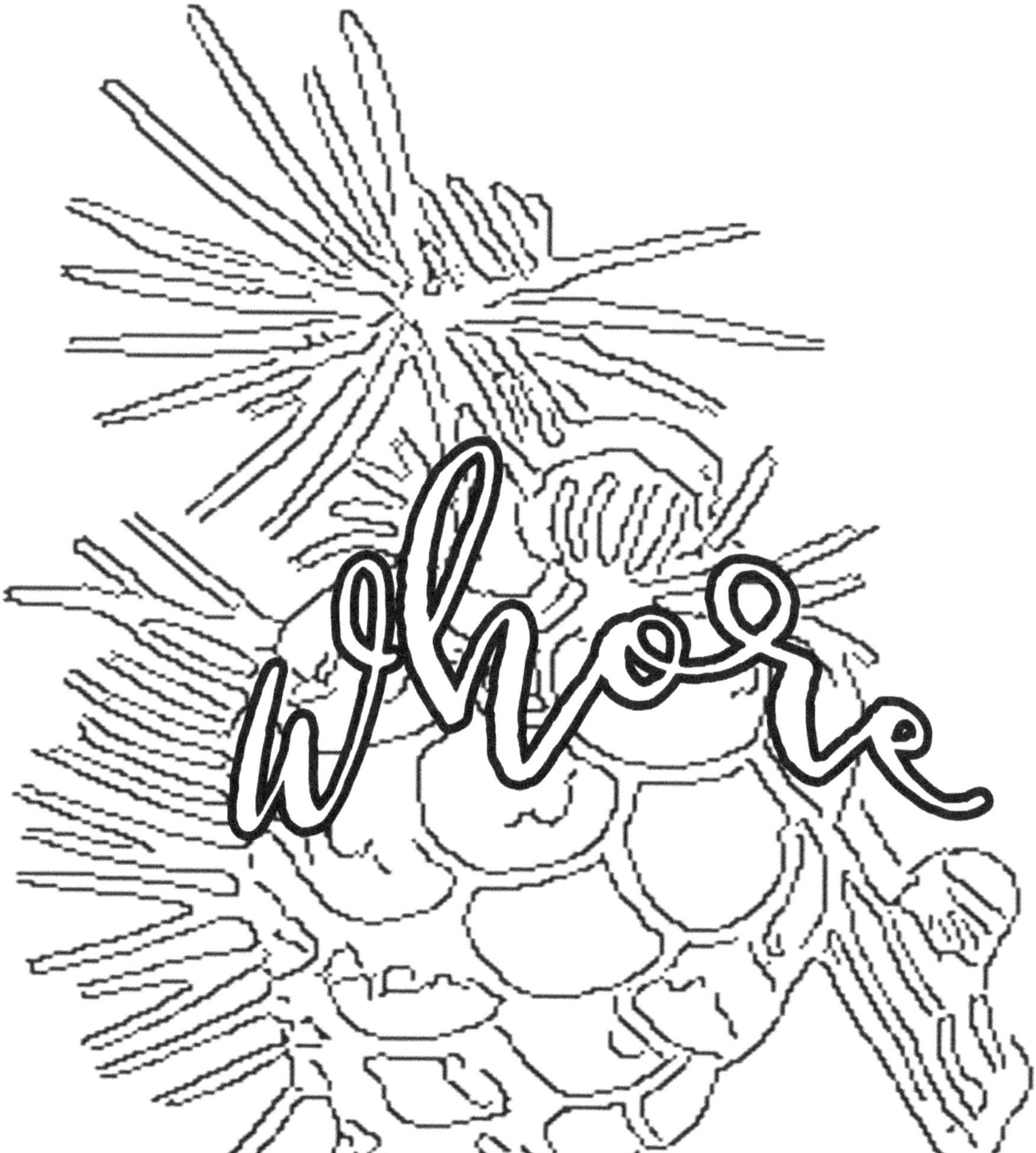
whore

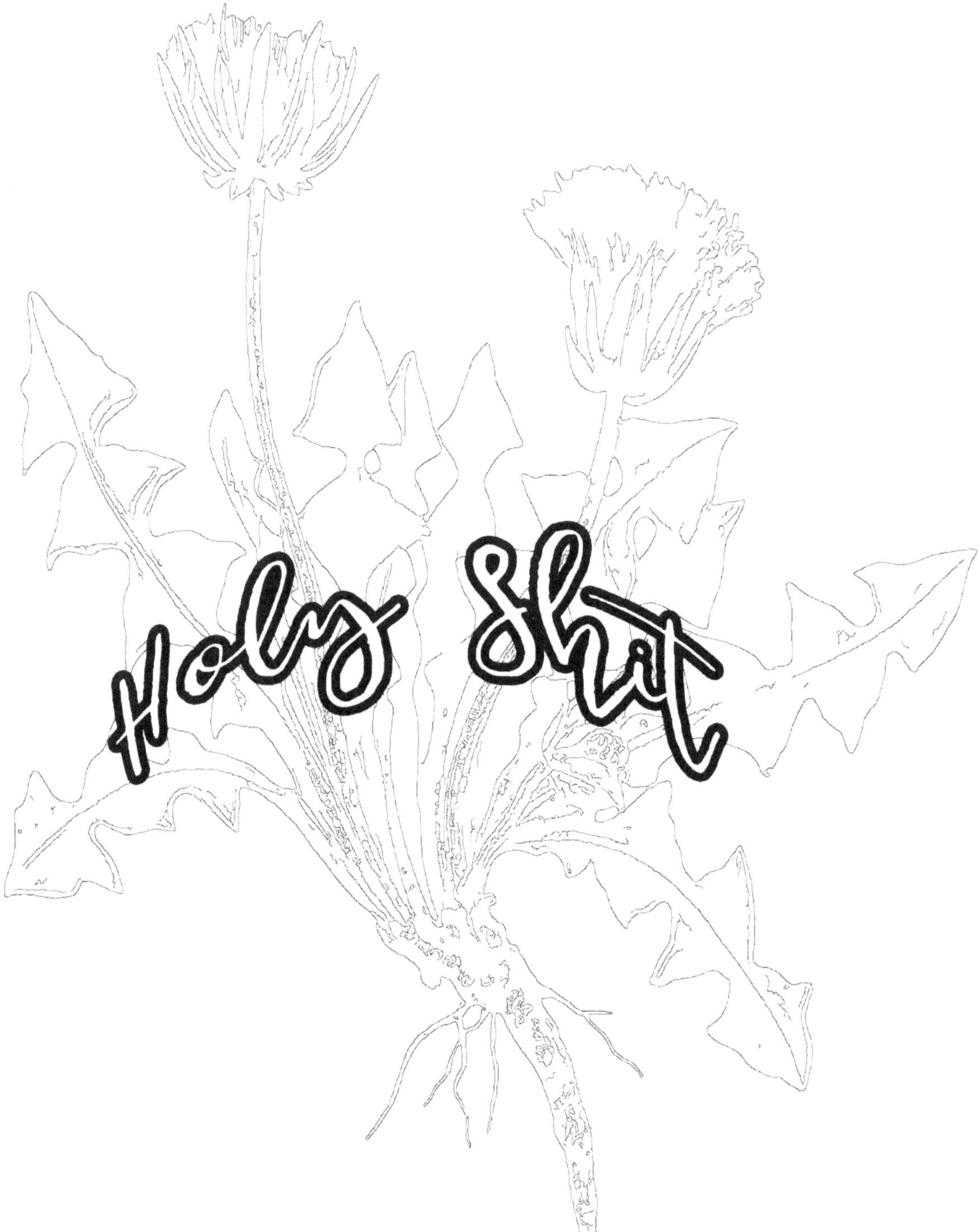
Holy Shit

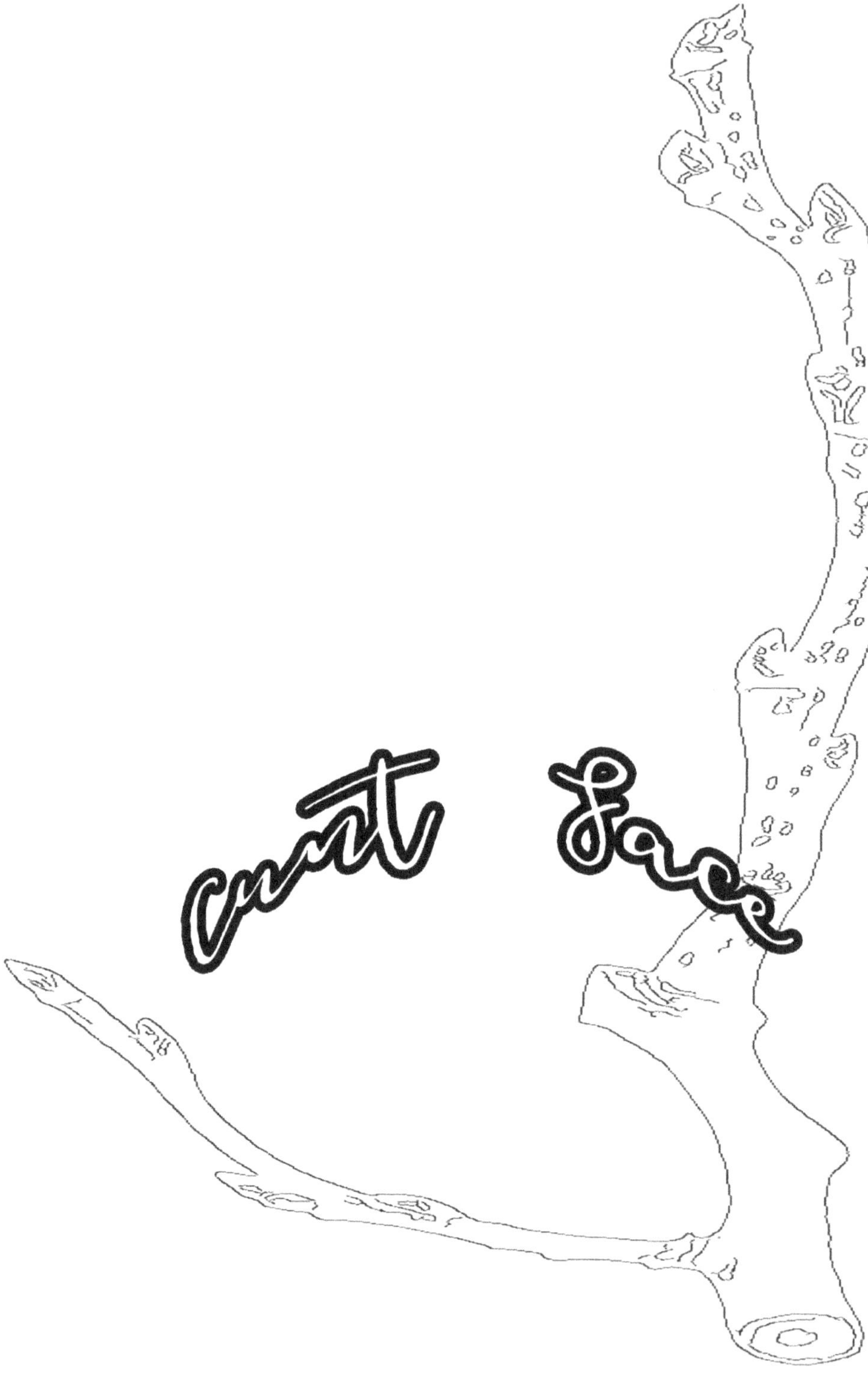
cunt face

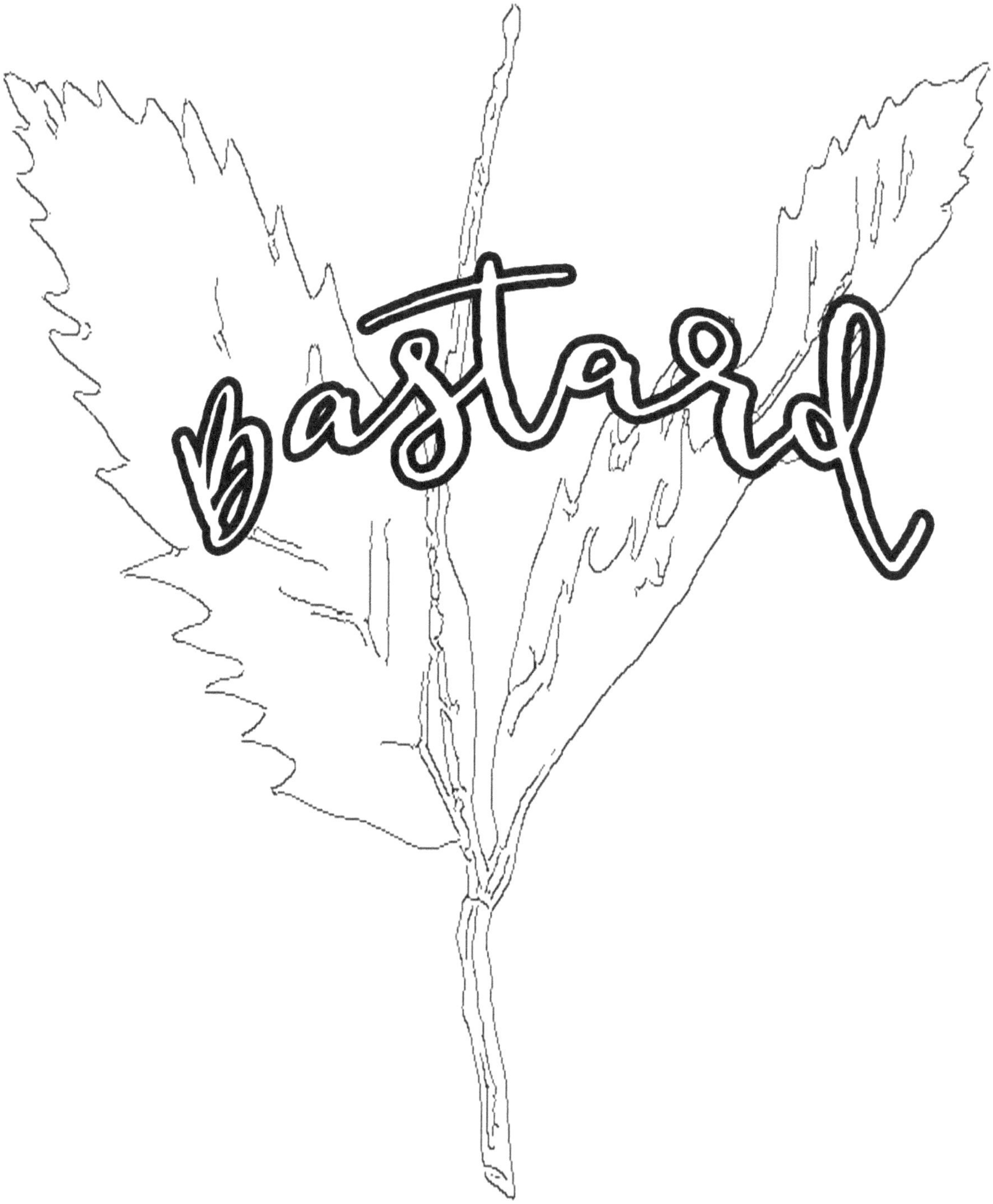
bastard

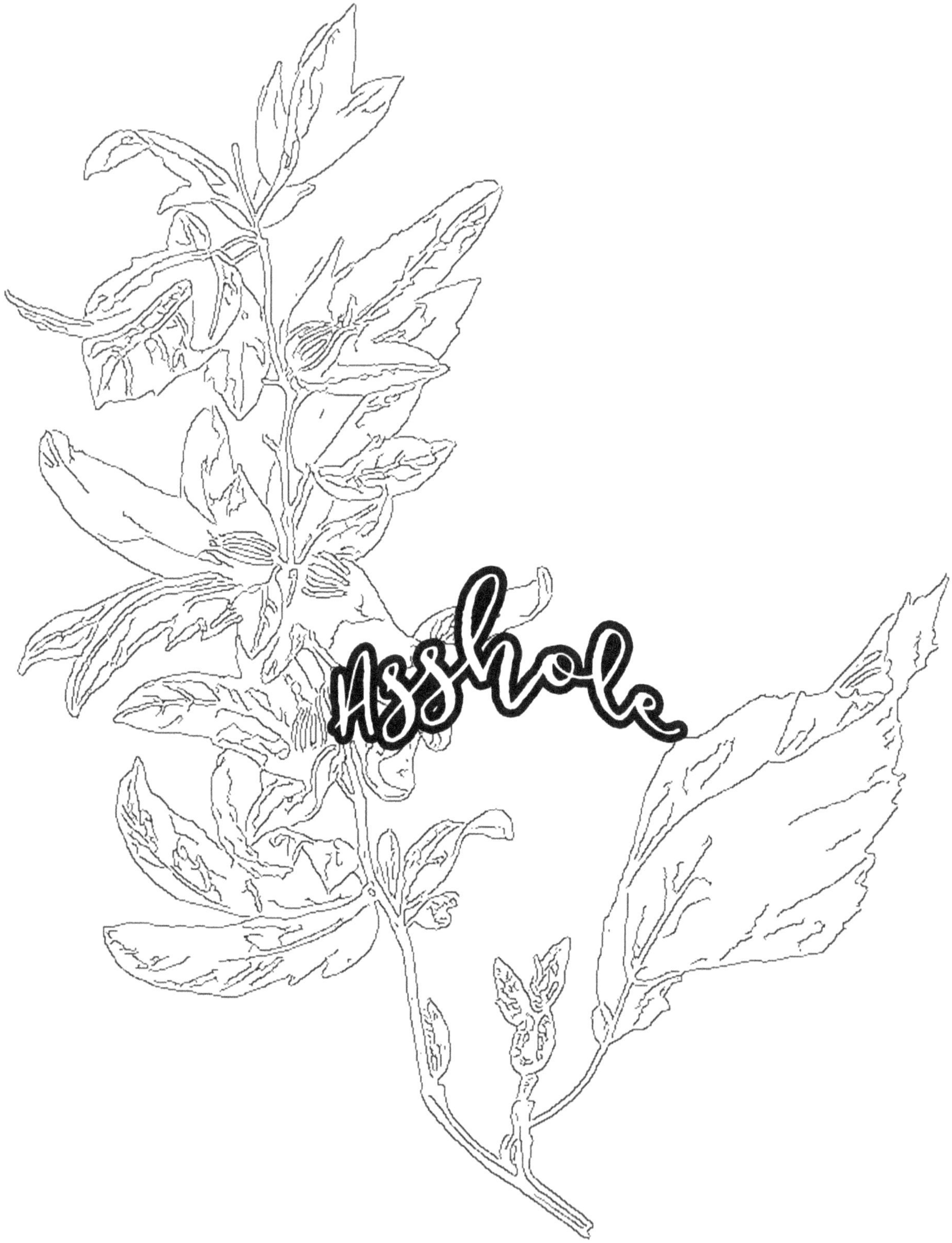
Asshole

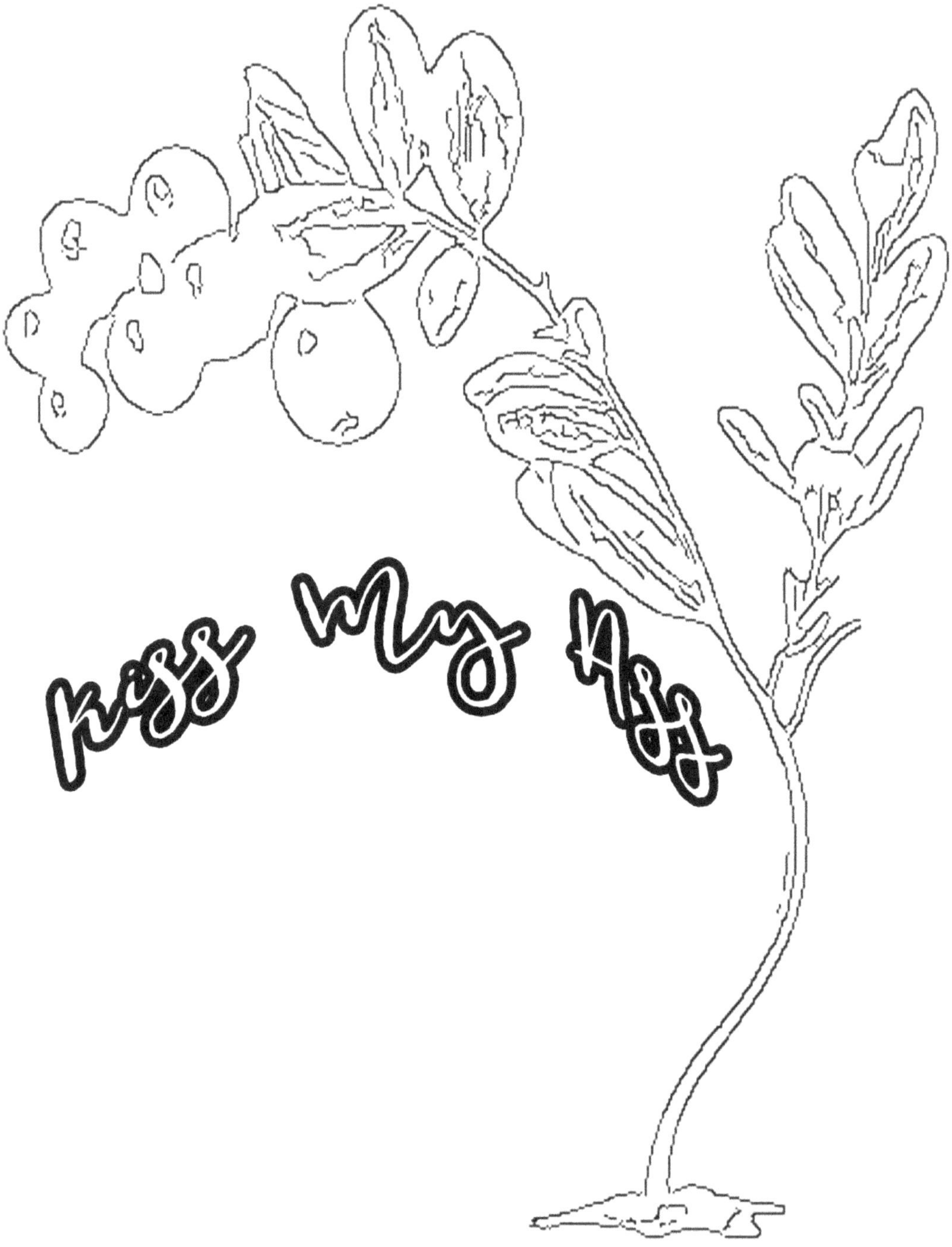
Kiss My Ass

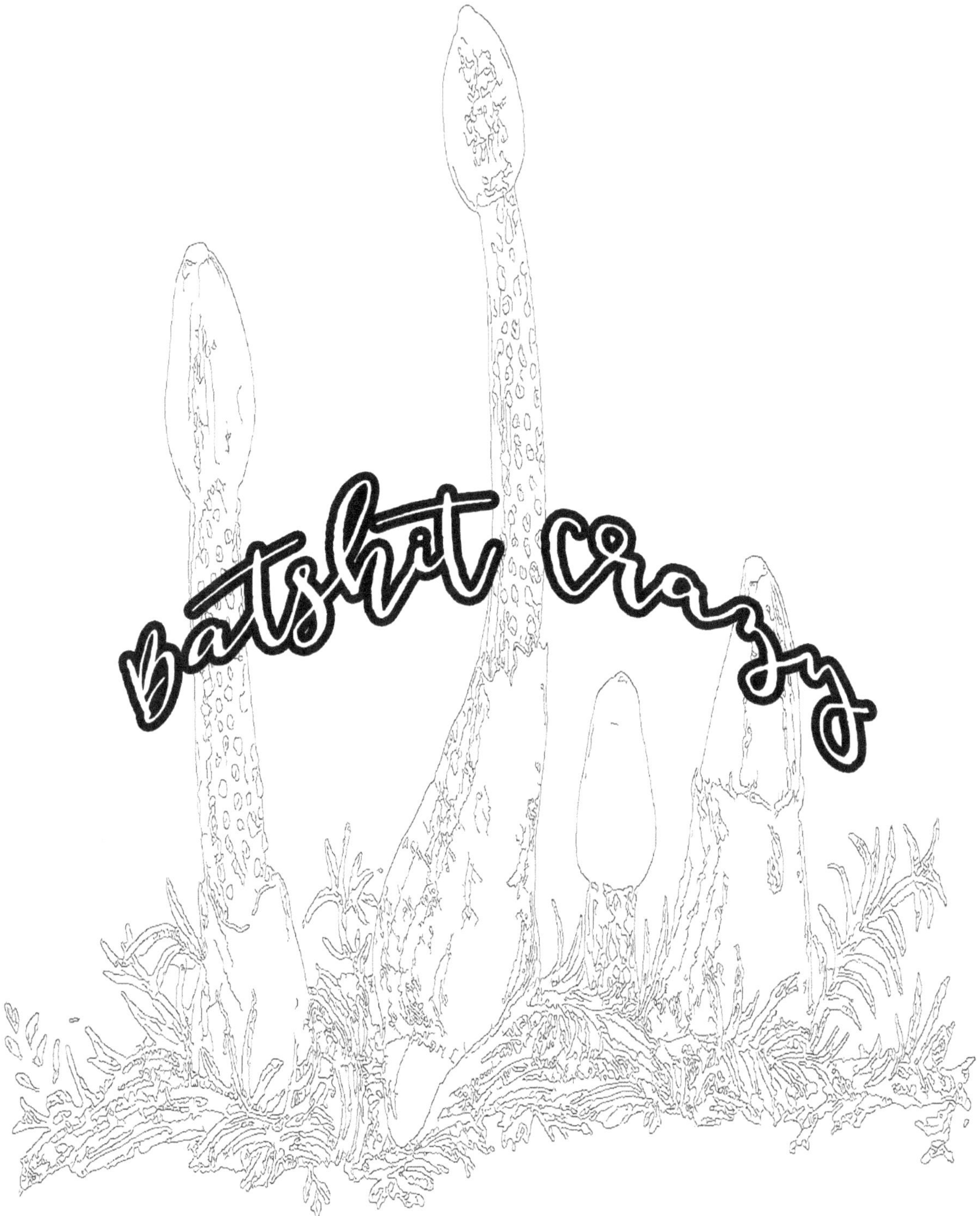
Batshit Crazy

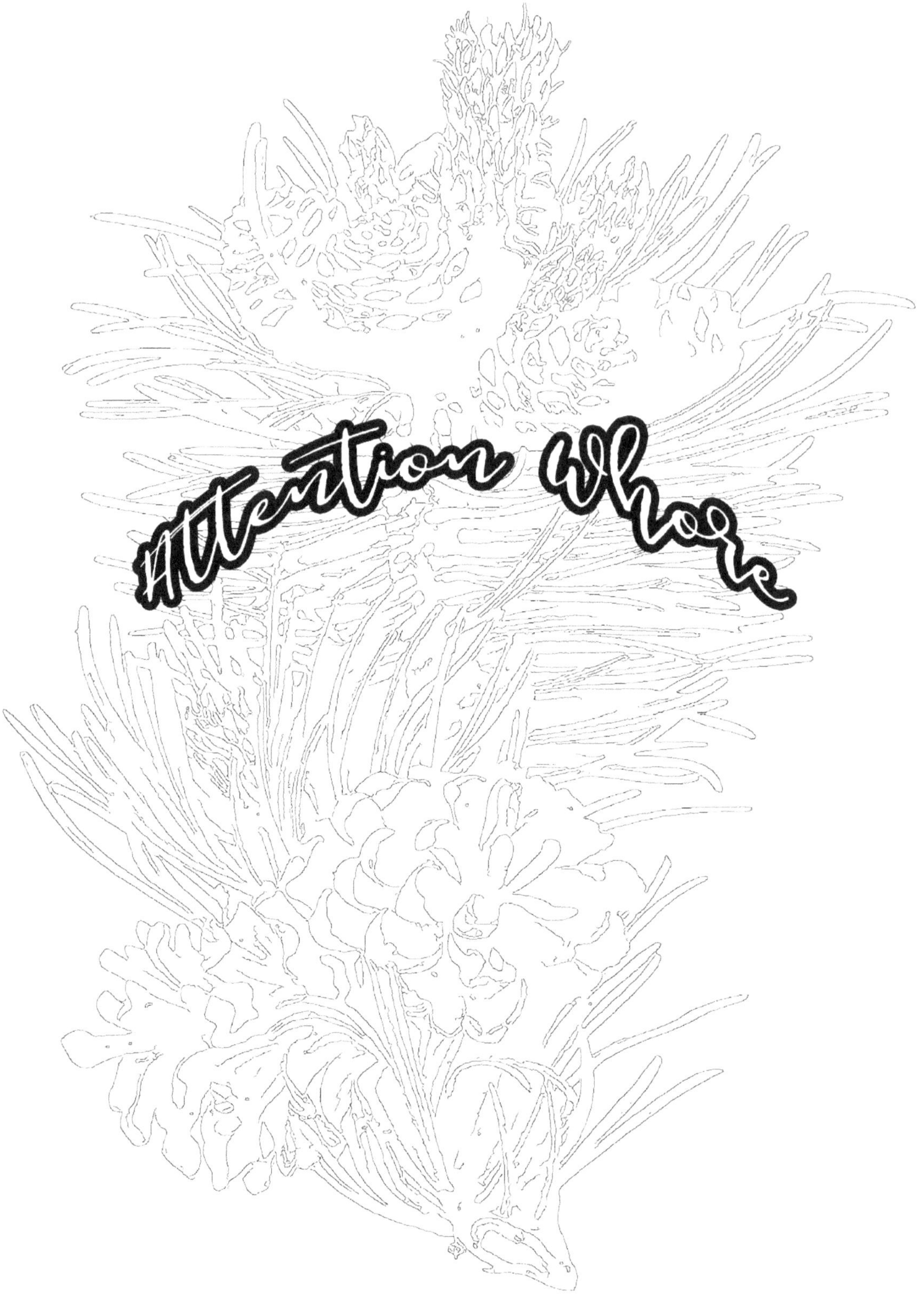
Attention Whore

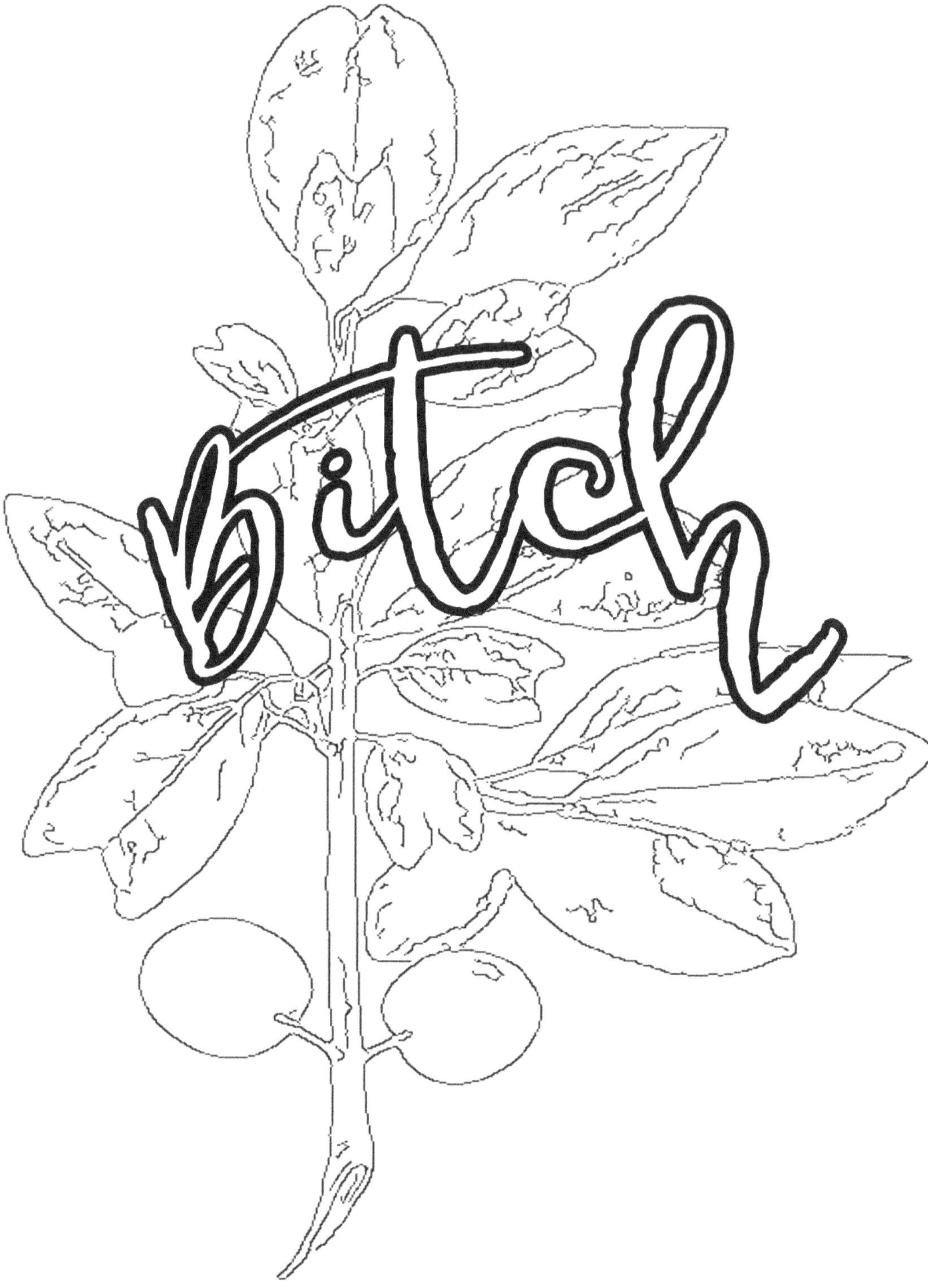
bitch

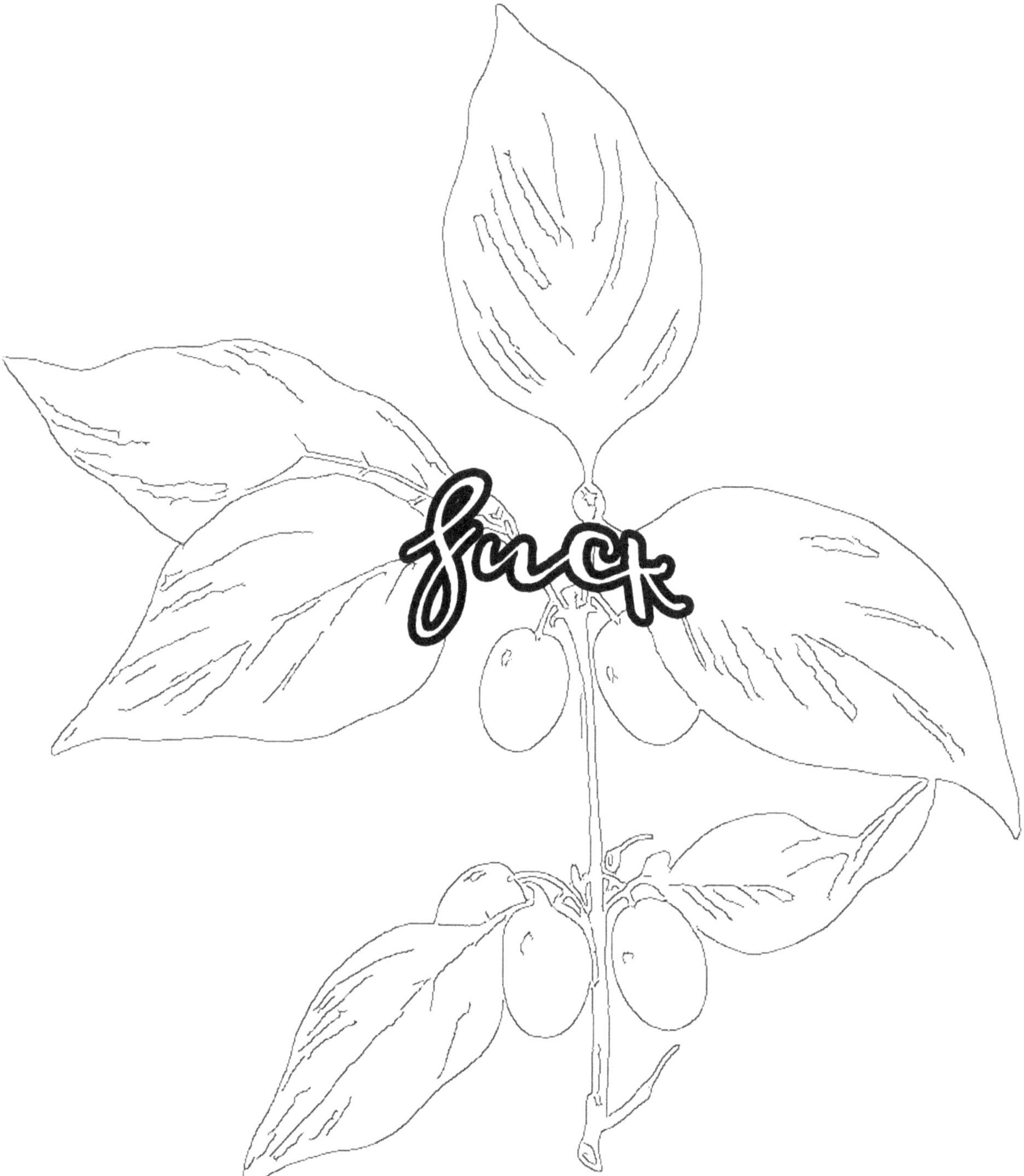
fuck

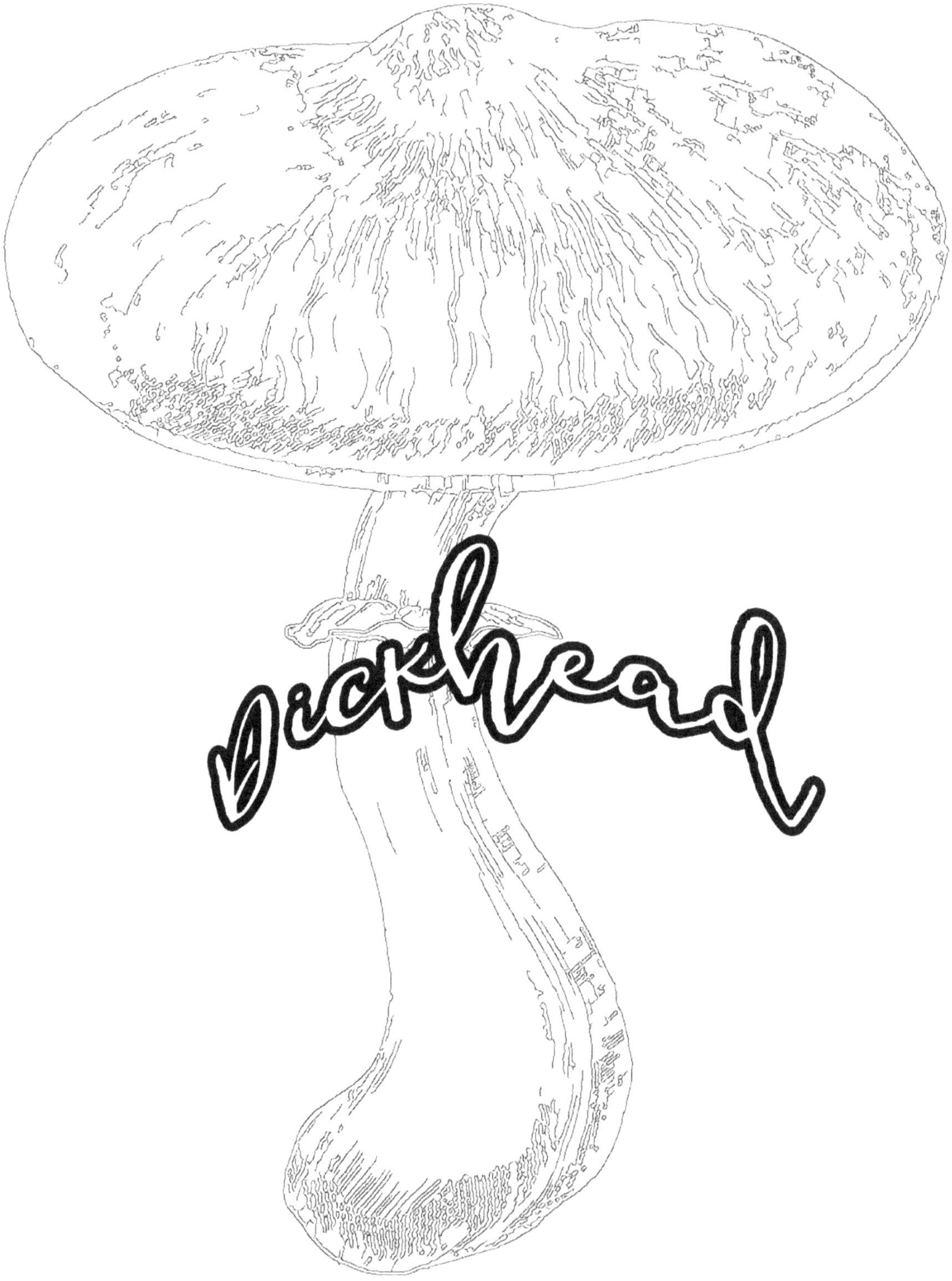
Dickhead

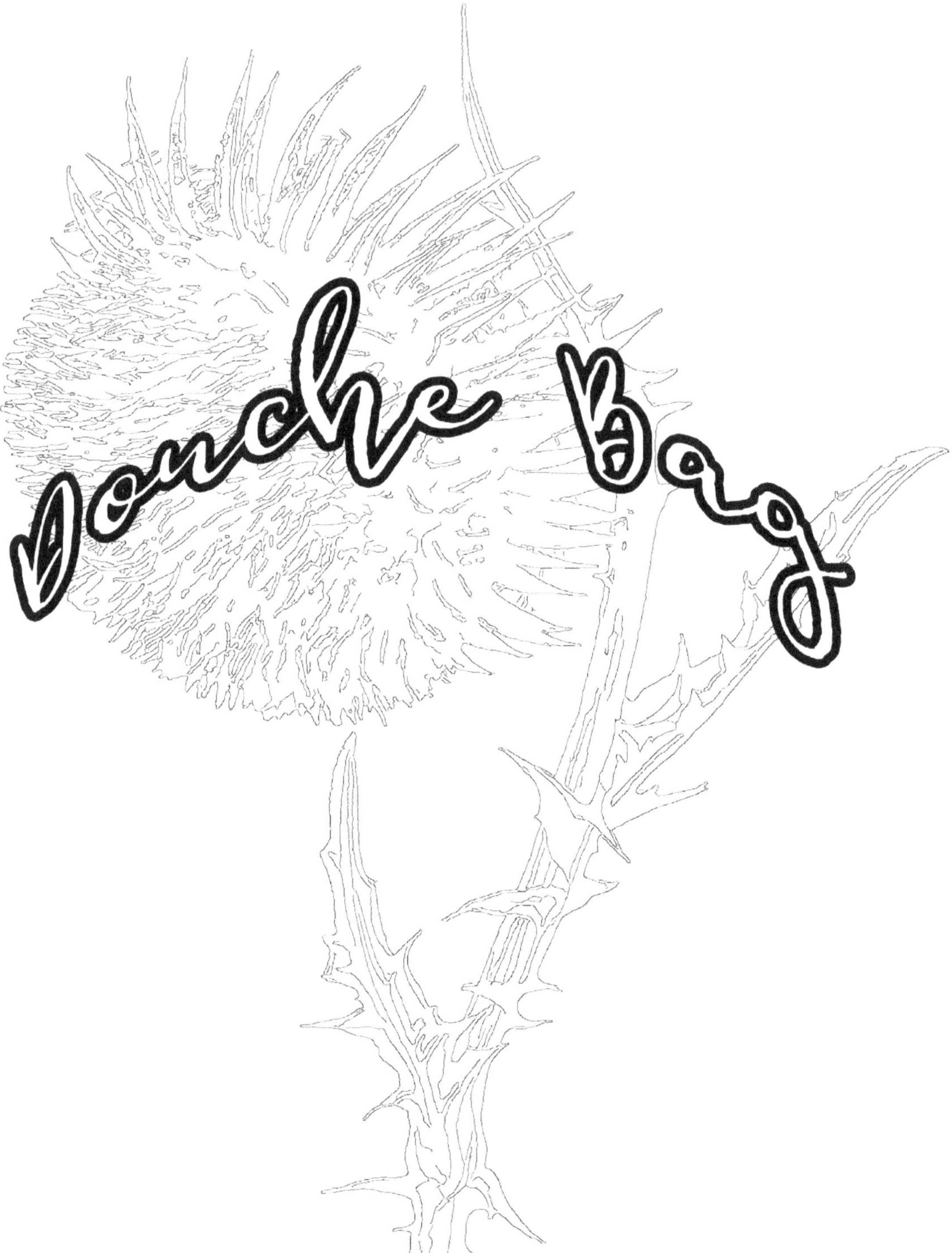
Douche Bag

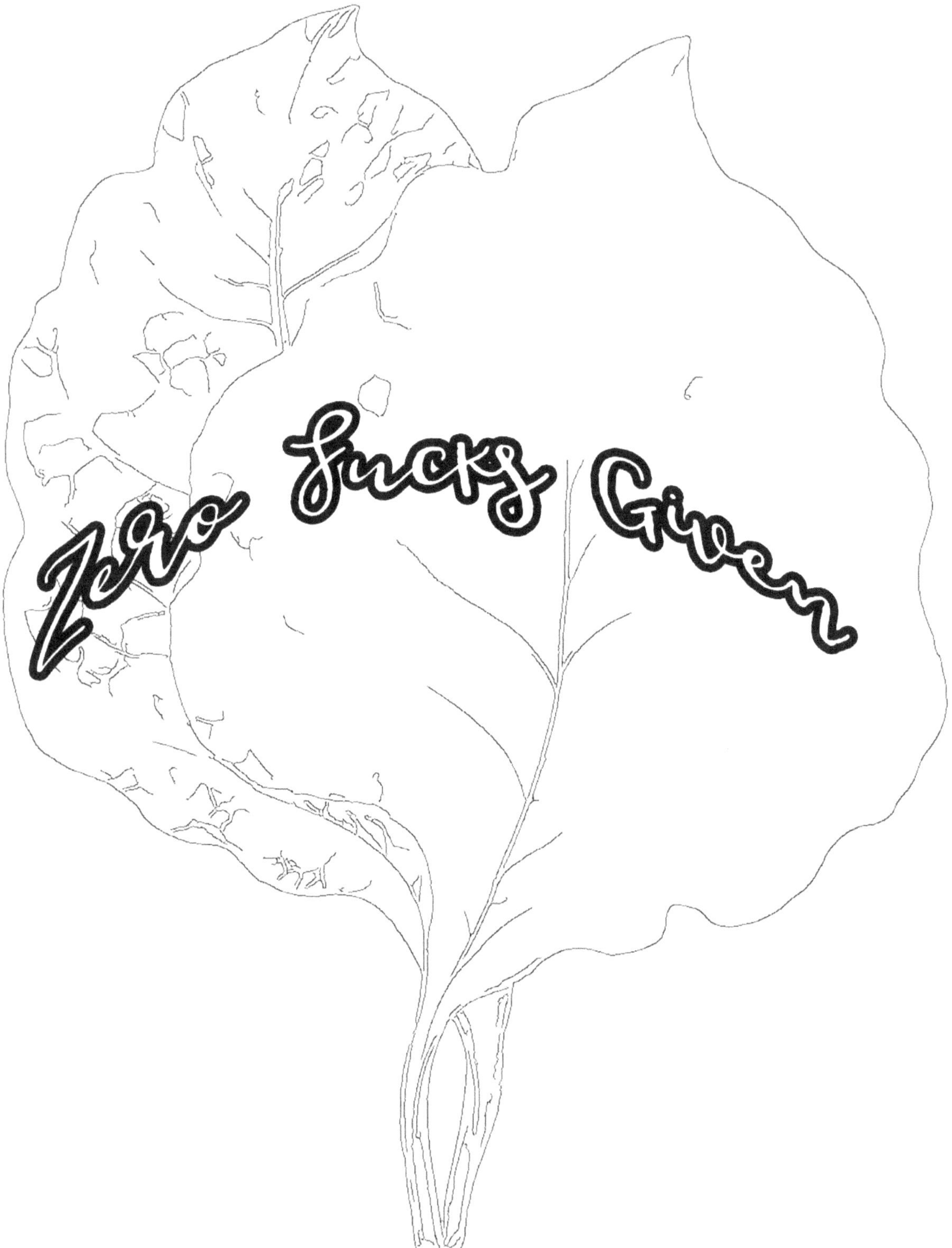
Zero Fucks Given

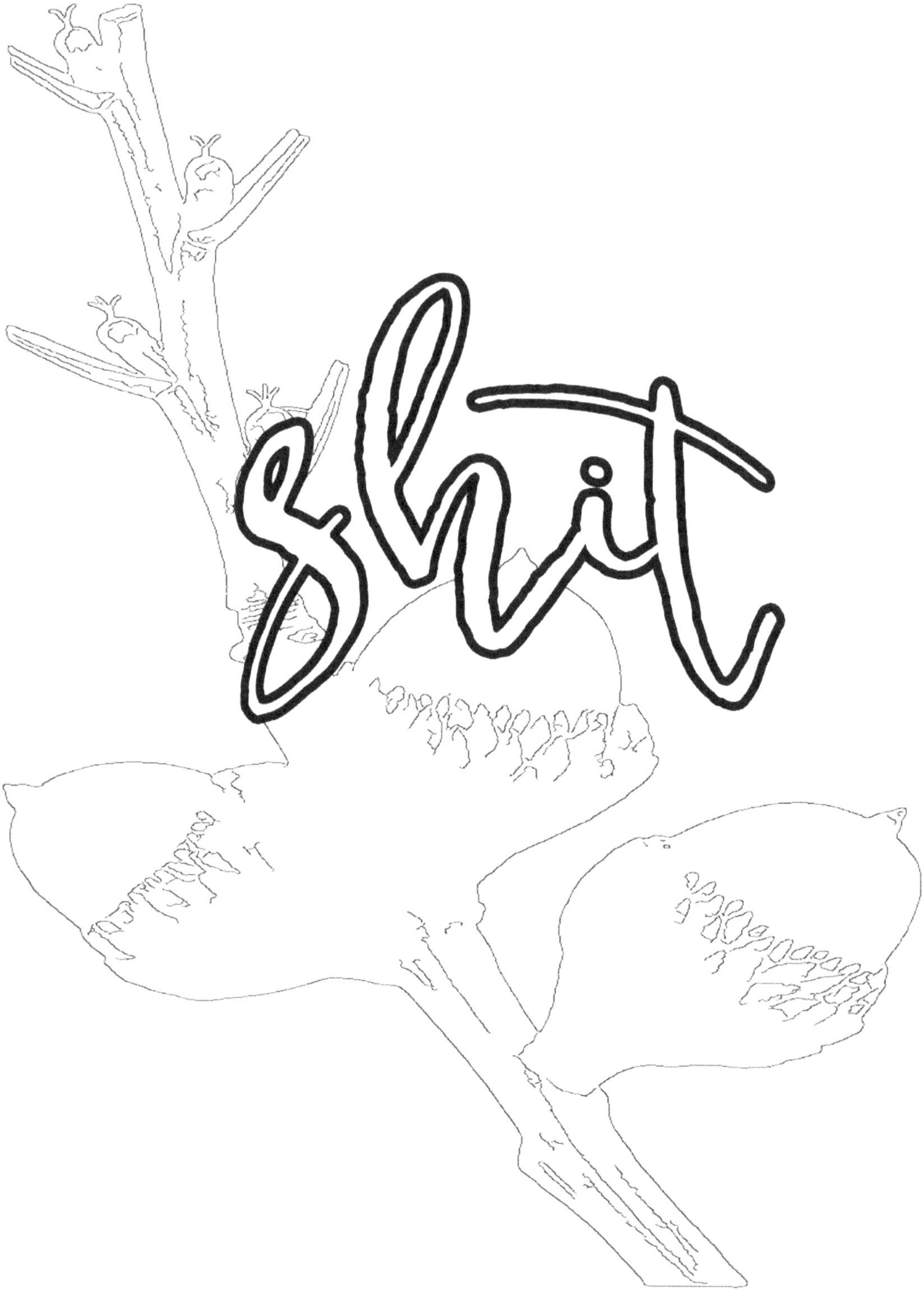
shit

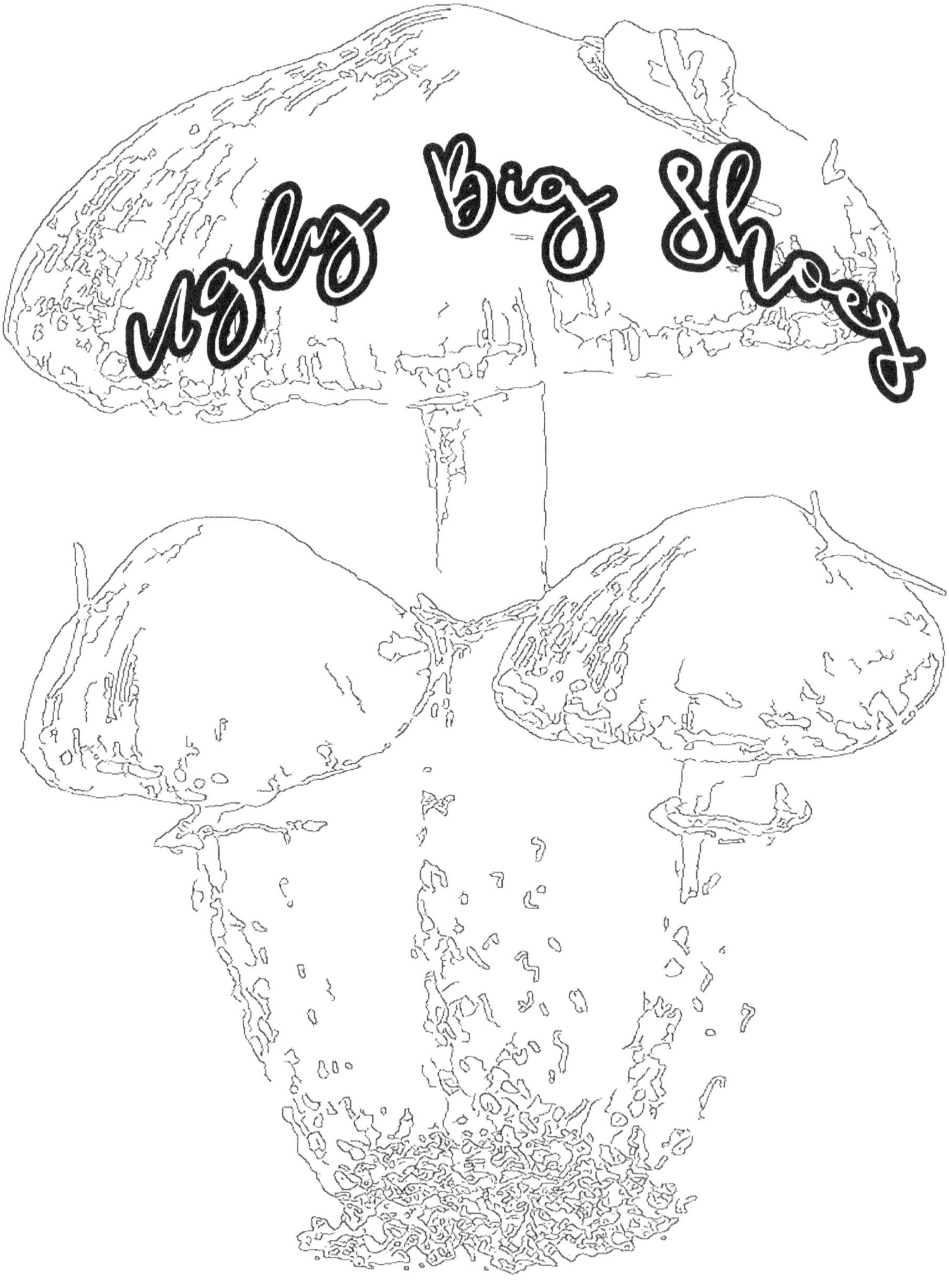
Ugly Big Shoes

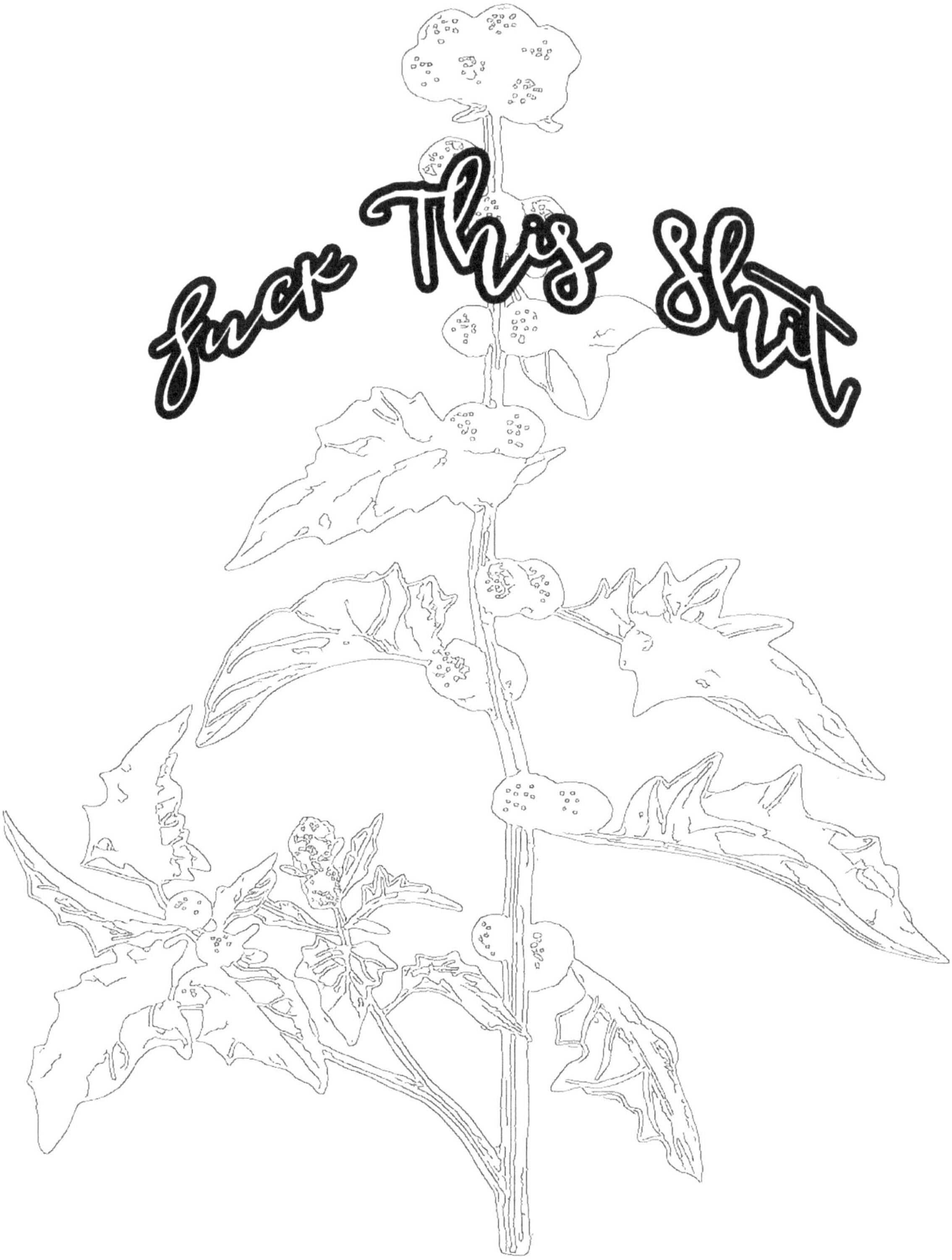
Fuck This Shit

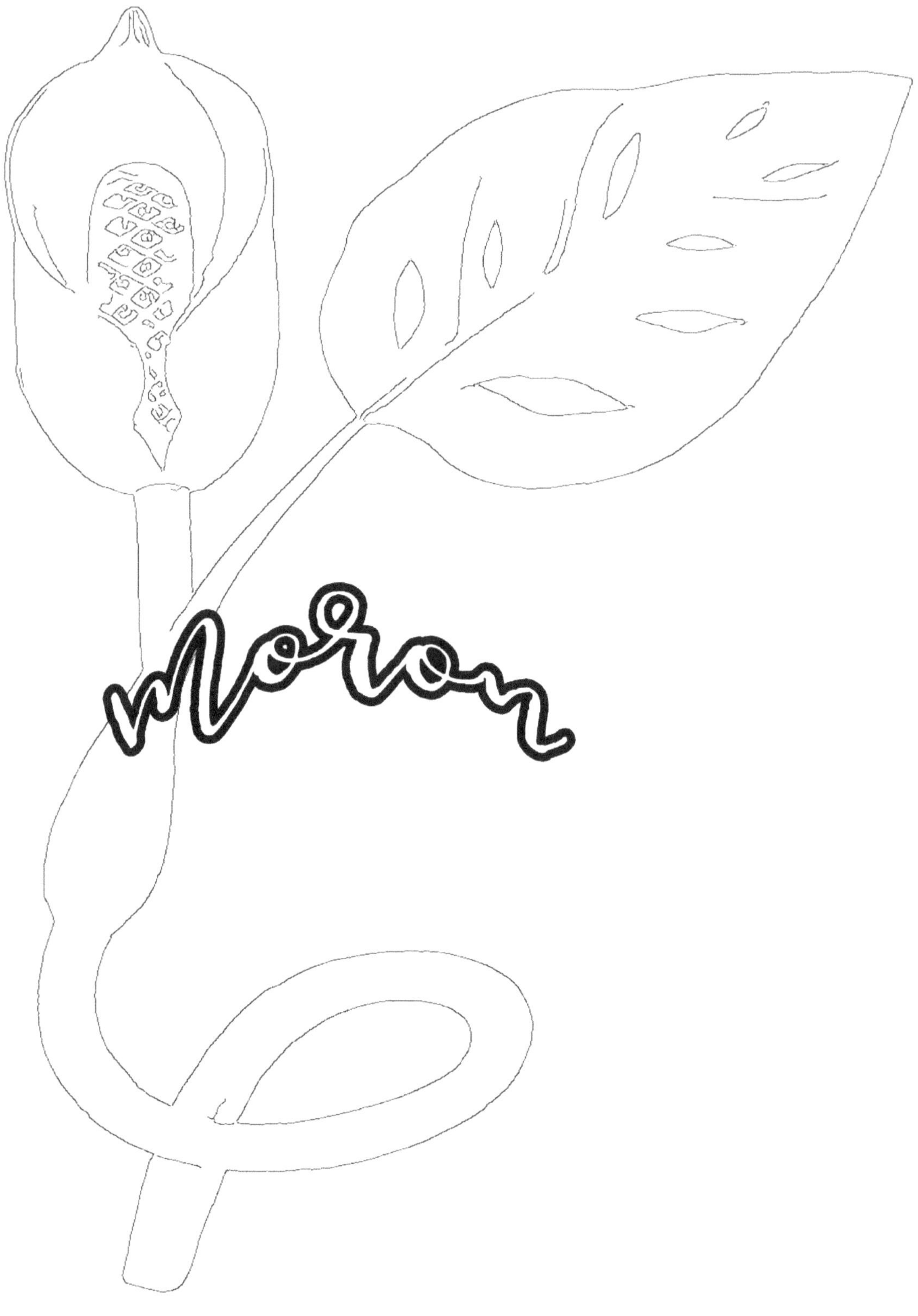
Moron

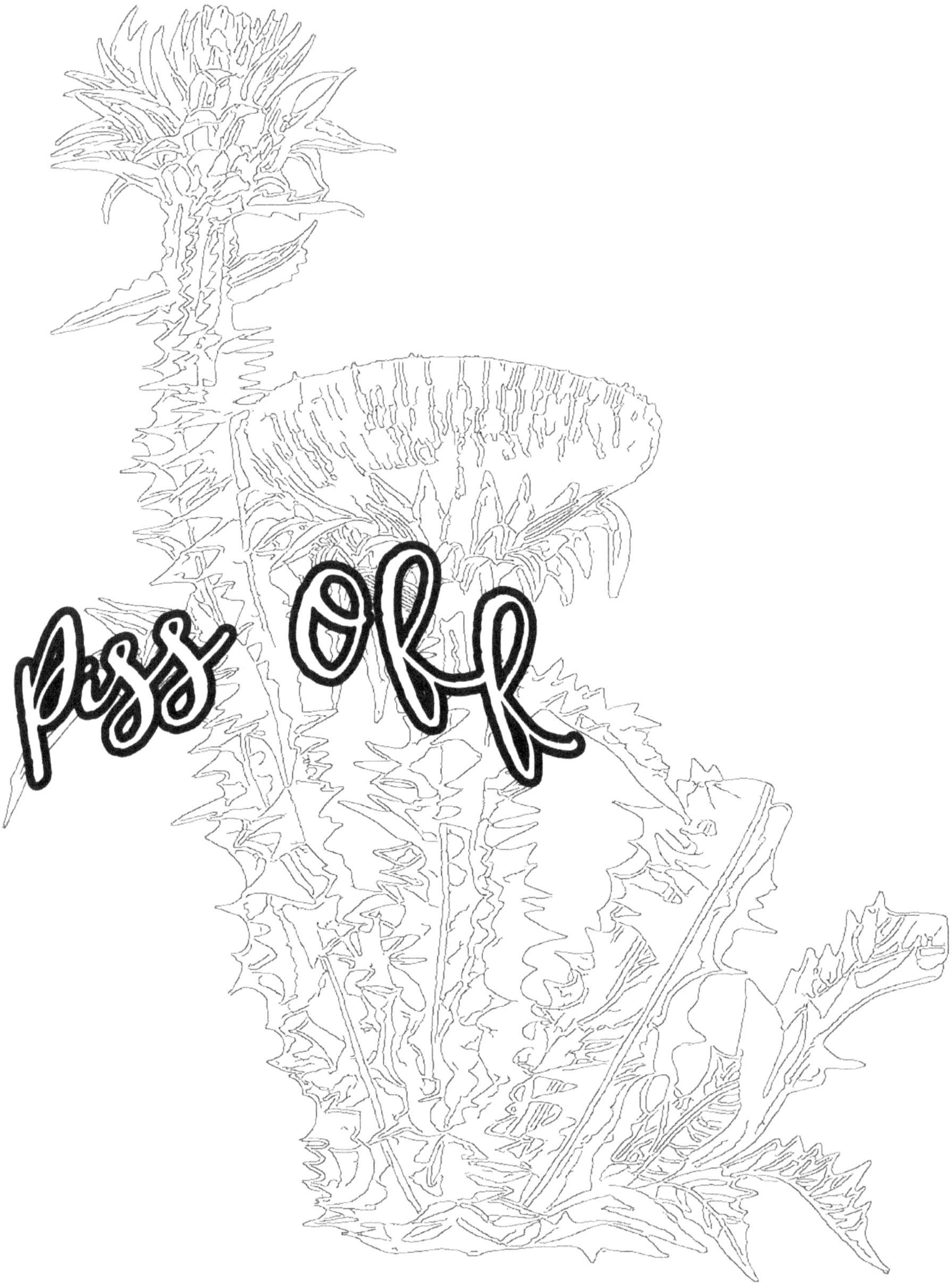
Piss Off

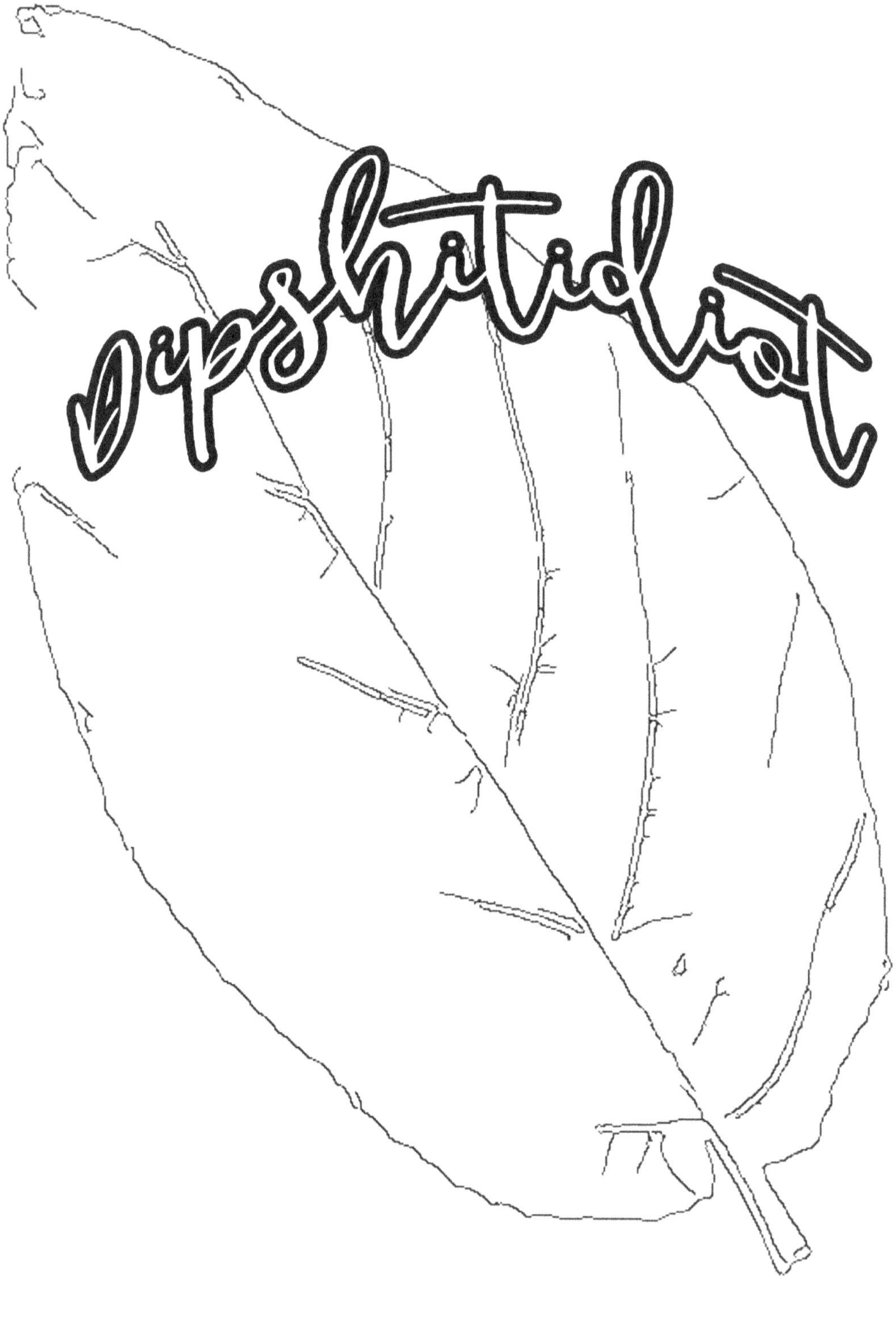
dipshitidiot

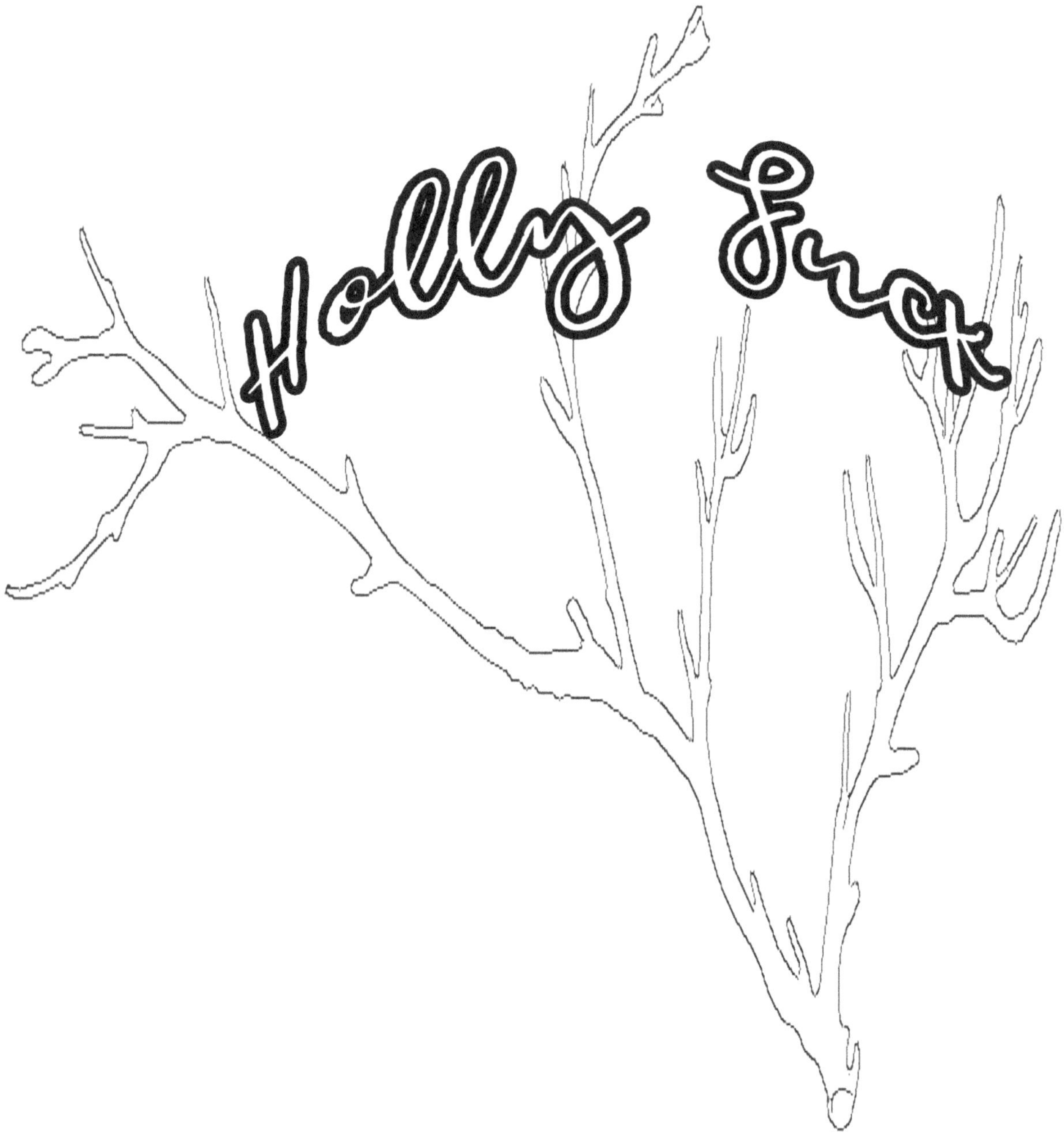
Holly Frost

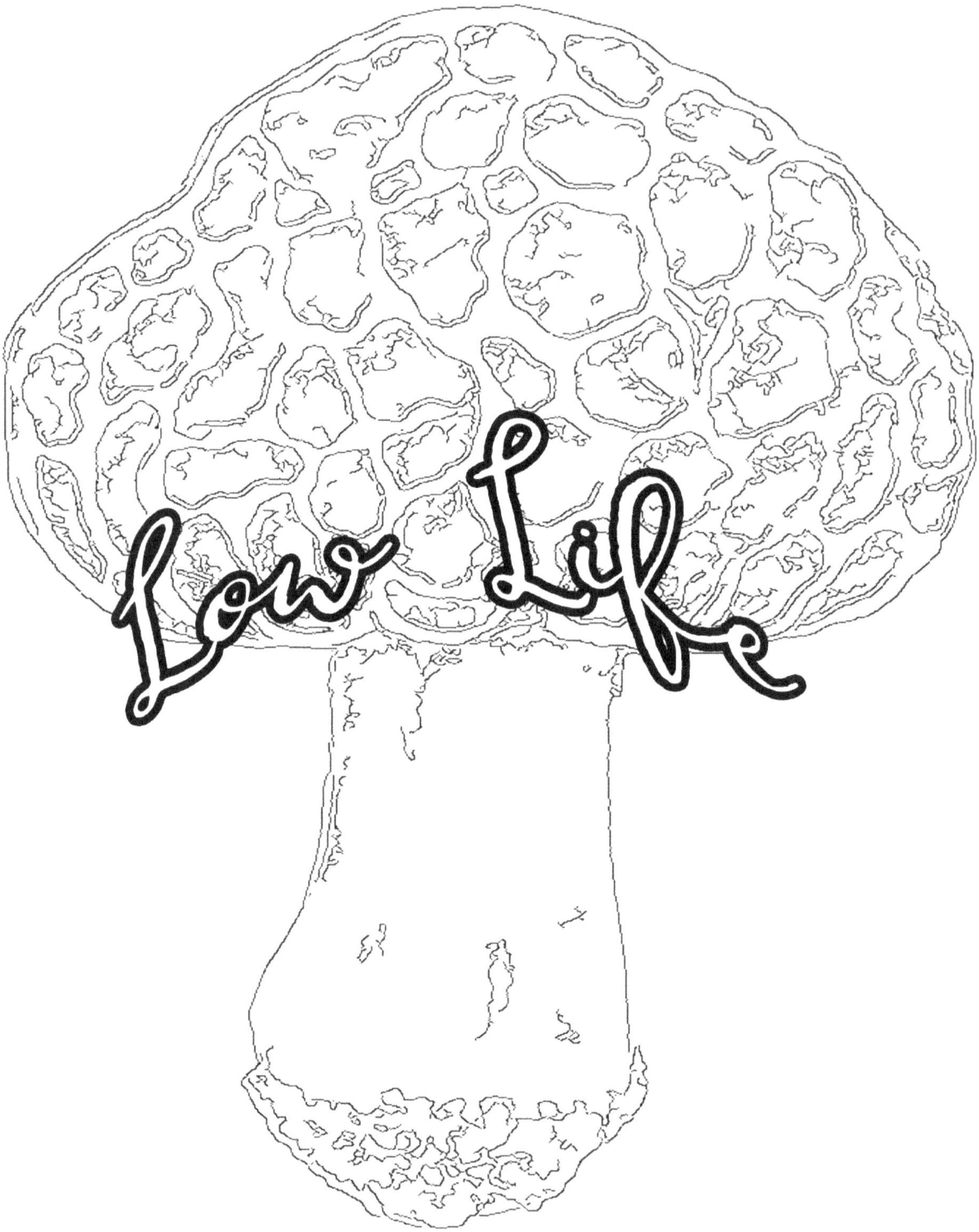
Low Life

www.ingramcontent.com/pod-product-compliance
Lightning Source LLC
Chambersburg PA
CBHW081619220526
45468CB00010B/2944
9781982031923